My **BIG** Picture Book of Phonics

My **BIG** Picture Book of Phonics

Teach Children to Learn and Write the Alphabet Faster than Ever!

Vernada Thomas

authorHOUSE®

AuthorHouse™ LLC
1663 Liberty Drive
Bloomington, IN 47403
www.authorhouse.com
Phone: 1-800-839-8640

Published by AuthorHouse   08/16/2013

ISBN: 978-1-4918-0328-8 (sc)
ISBN: 978-1-4918-0327-1 (e)

Library of Congress Control Number: 2013911488

Any people depicted in stock imagery provided by Thinkstock are models, and such images are being used for illustrative purposes only.
Certain stock imagery © Thinkstock.

This book is printed on acid-free paper.

Because of the dynamic nature of the Internet, any web addresses or links contained in this book may have changed since publication and may no longer be valid. The views expressed in this work are solely those of the author and do not necessarily reflect the views of the publisher, and the publisher hereby disclaims any responsibility for them.

Practice daily for 15 minutes.

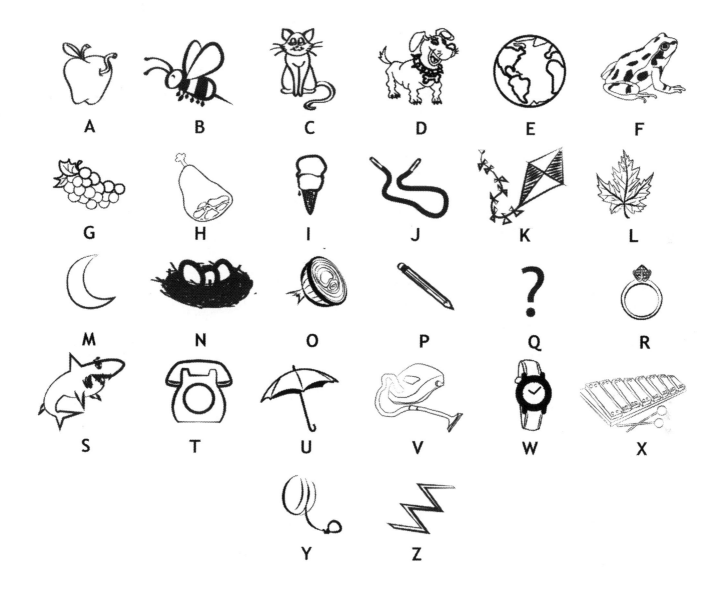

A
B
C
D
E
F

G
H
I
J
K
L

M
N
O
P
Q
R

S
T
U
V
W
X

Y
Z

In order for the child to memorize the letter and sound, be sure to have him or her point to each letter as they practice it.

Can you tell me what letter this is?

Have the child repeat this twice.

What begins with the Letter A ?

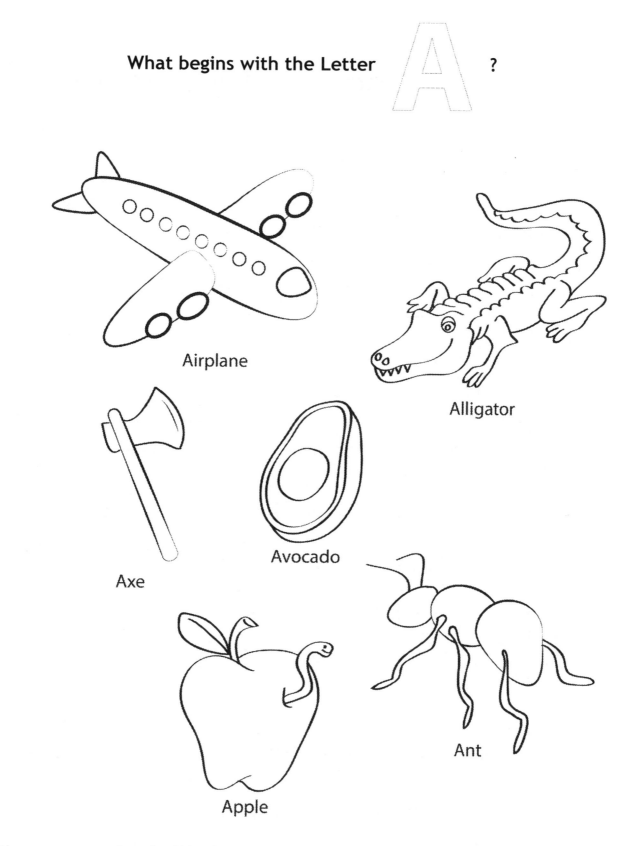

Airplane

Alligator

Axe

Avocado

Apple

Ant

Say the name out loud of each picture and listen carefully to the vowel sound of the words that begin with the letter "A." Color it.

Can you tell me what letter this is?

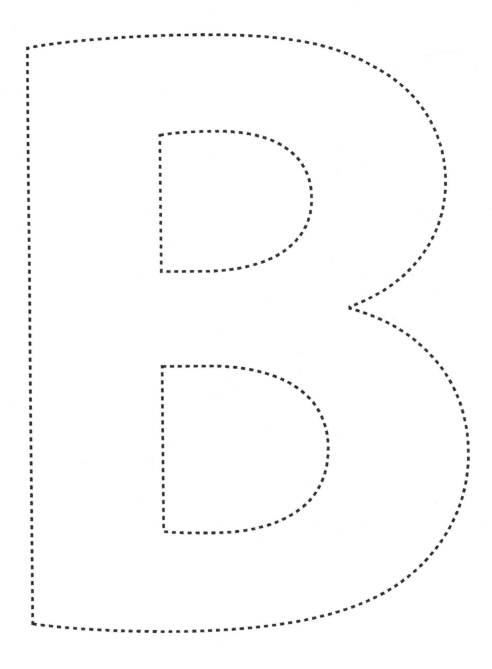

Have the child repeat this twice.

What begins with the Letter B ?

Boots

Balloon

Bee

Basket

Bird

Book

Ball

Bat

Say the name out loud of each picture and listen carefully to the consonant sound
of the words that begin with the letter "B." Color it.

Can you tell me what letter this is?

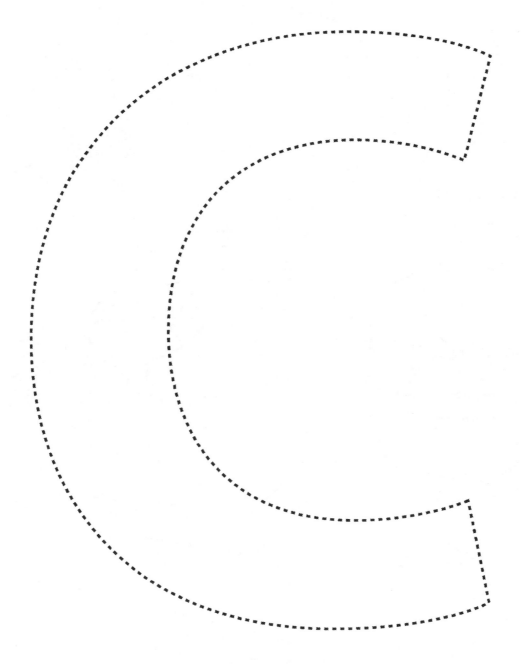

Have the child repeat this twice.

What begins with the Letter C ?

Cow

Castle

Cat

Carrot

Cake

Can

Say the name out loud of each picture and listen carefully to the consonant sound of the words that begin with the letter "C." Color it.

Can you tell me what letter this is?

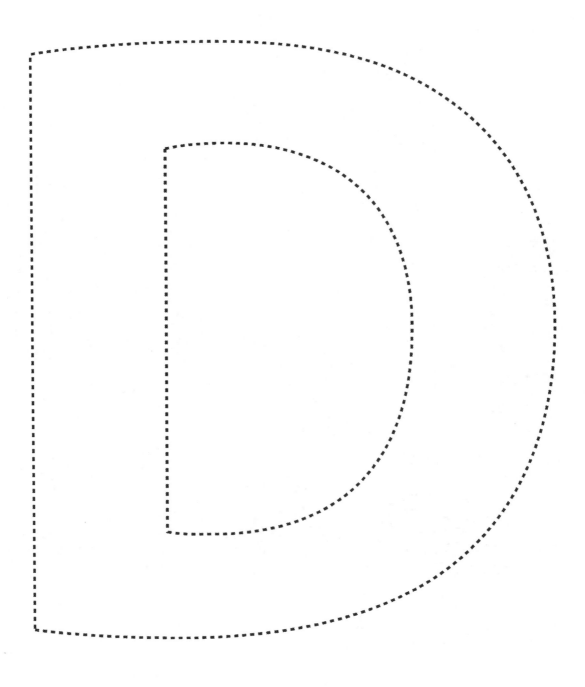

Have the child repeat this twice.

What begins with the Letter D ?

Duck

Dog

Dinosaur

Dragon

Dolphin

Deer

Say the name out loud of each picture and listen carefully to the consonant sound of the words that begin with the letter "D." Color it.

Can you tell me what letter this is?

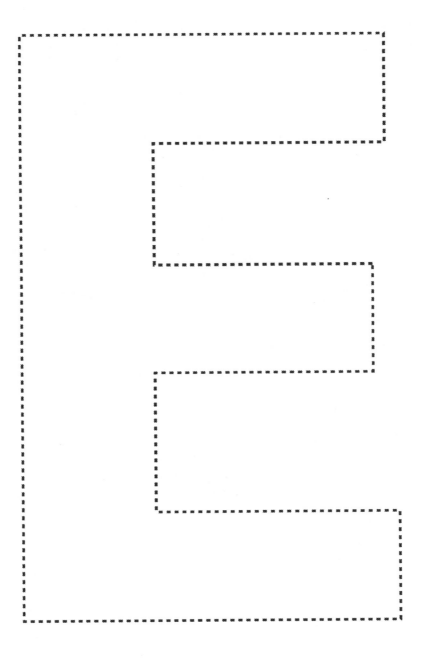

Have the child repeat this twice.

What begins with the Letter E ?

Elephant

Earth

18 Eighteen

Eye

Egg

8 Eight

Eagle

Say the name out loud of each picture and listen carefully to the vowel sound of the words that begin with the letter "E." Color it.

Can you tell me what letter this is?

Have the child repeat this twice.

What begins with the Letter F ?

Fork

Frog

Fan

Flag

Fire

Fly

Say the name out loud of each picture and listen carefully to the consonant sound of the words that begin with the letter "F." Color it.

13

Can you tell me what letter this is?

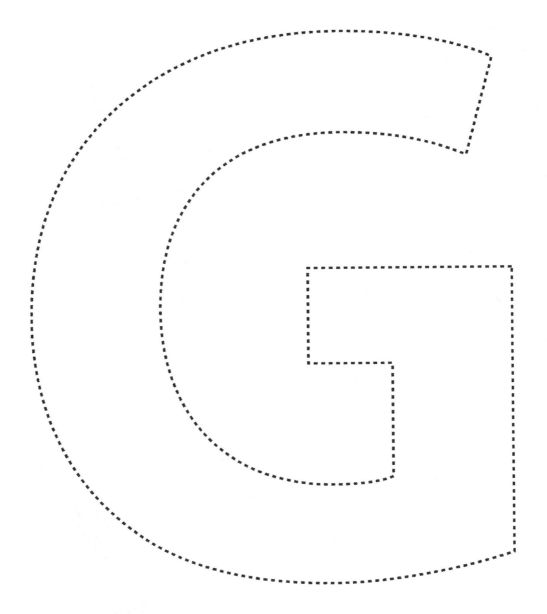

Have the child repeat this twice.

What begins with the Letter G ?

Gift

Grapes

Gorilla

Guitar

Girl

Goat

Say the name out loud of each picture and listen carefully to the consonant sound of the words that begin with the letter "G." Color it.

Can you tell me what letter this is?

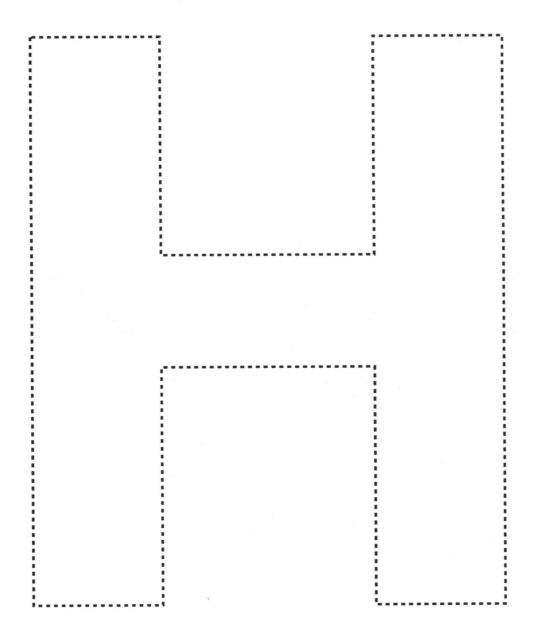

Have the child repeat this twice.

What begins with the Letter H ?

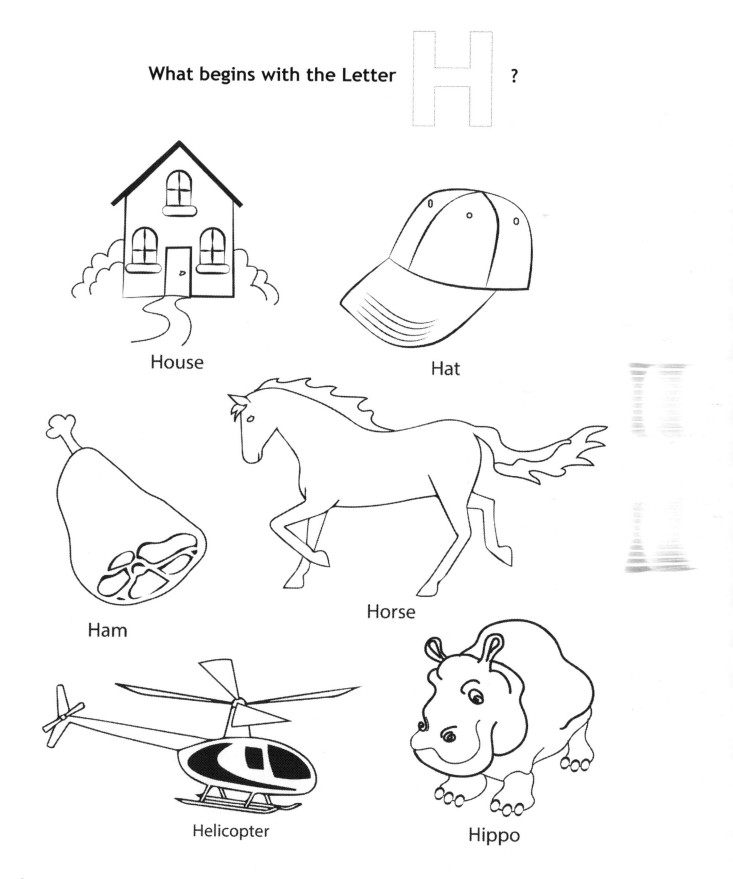

House

Hat

Ham

Horse

Helicopter

Hippo

Say the name out loud of each picture and listen carefully to the consonant sound of the words that begin with the letter "H." Color it.

Can you tell me what letter this is?

Have the child repeat this twice.

What begins with the Letter ☐ **?**

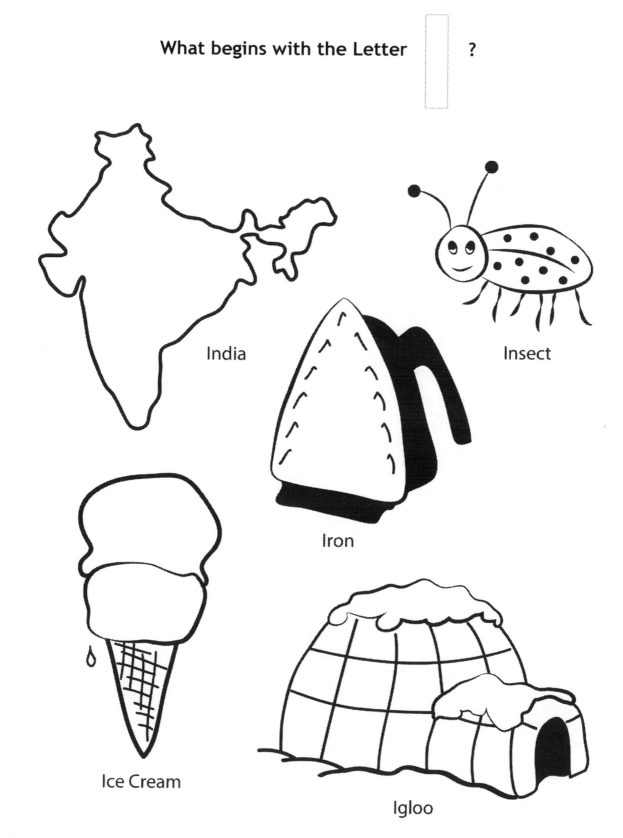

India

Insect

Iron

Ice Cream

Igloo

Say the name out loud of each picture and listen carefully to the vowel sound of the words that begin with the letter "I." Color it.

Can you tell me what letter this is?

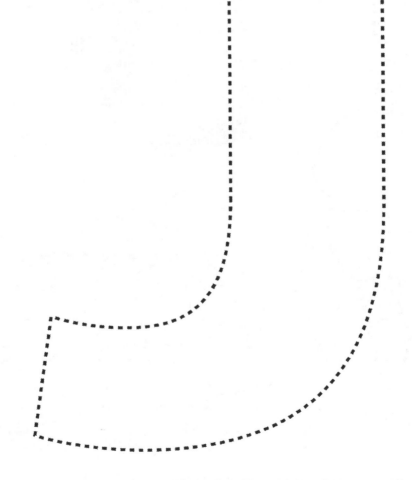

Have the child repeat this twice.

What begins with the Letter J ?

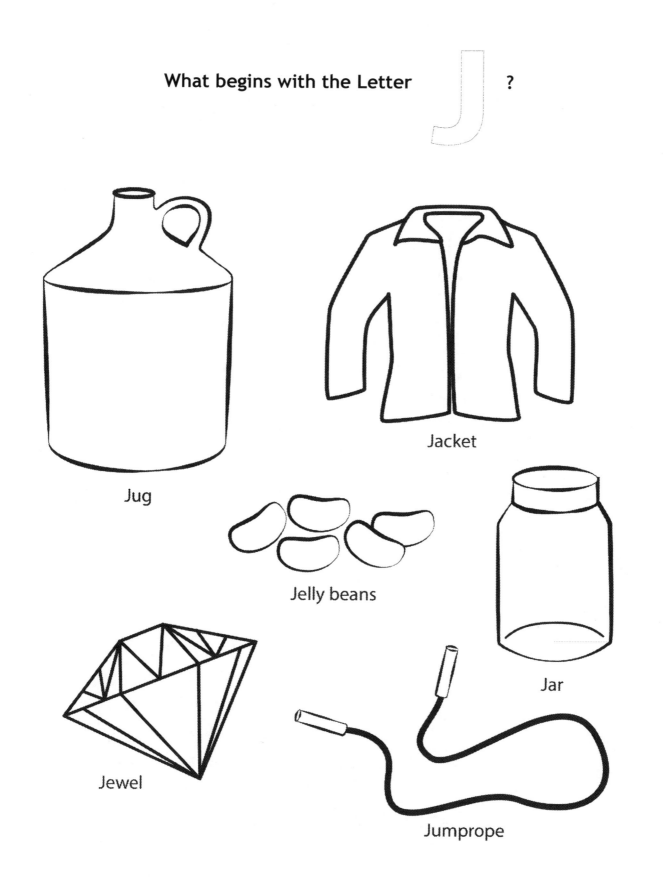

Jug

Jacket

Jelly beans

Jar

Jewel

Jumprope

Say the name out loud of each picture and listen carefully to the consonant sound of the words that begin with the letter "J." Color it.

Can you tell me what letter this is?

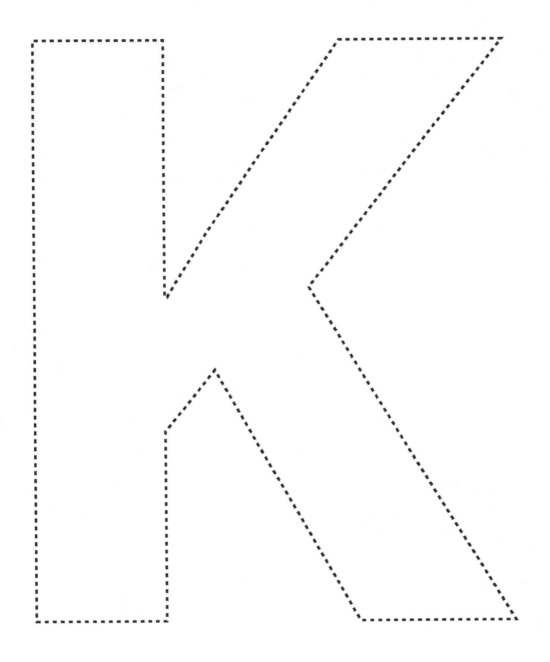

Have the child repeat this twice.

What begins with the Letter K ?

Key

Kazoo

Kleenex

Kite

Kangaroo

Kayak

Say the name out loud of each picture and listen carefully to the consonant sound of the words that begin with the letter "K." Color it.

Can you tell me what letter this is?

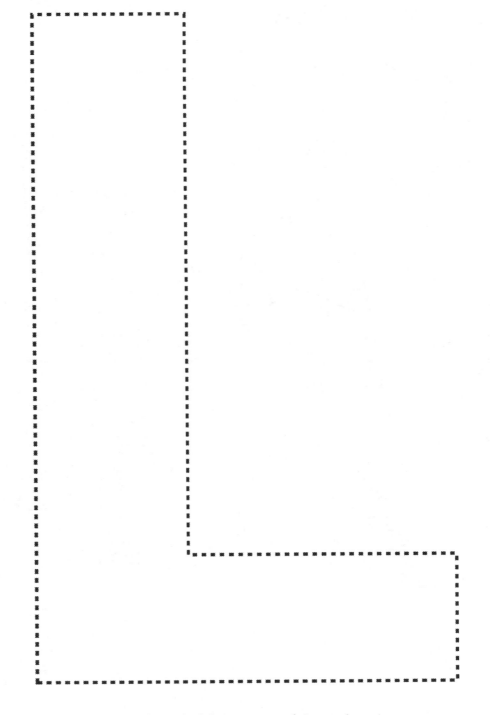

Have the child repeat this twice.

What begins with the Letter L **?**

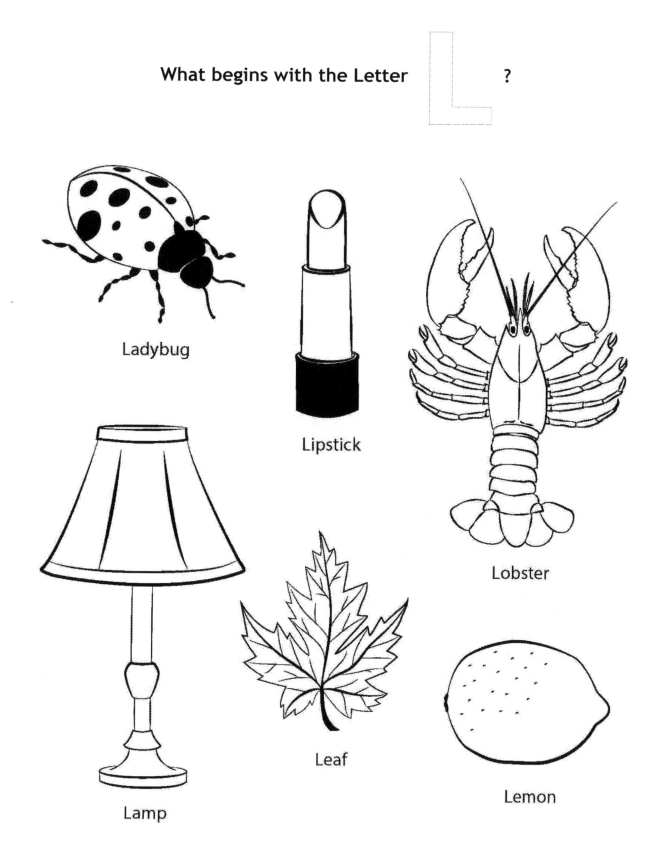

Ladybug

Lipstick

Lobster

Lamp

Leaf

Lemon

Say the name out loud of each picture and listen carefully to the consonant sound of the words that begin with the letter "L." Color it.

Can you tell me what letter this is?

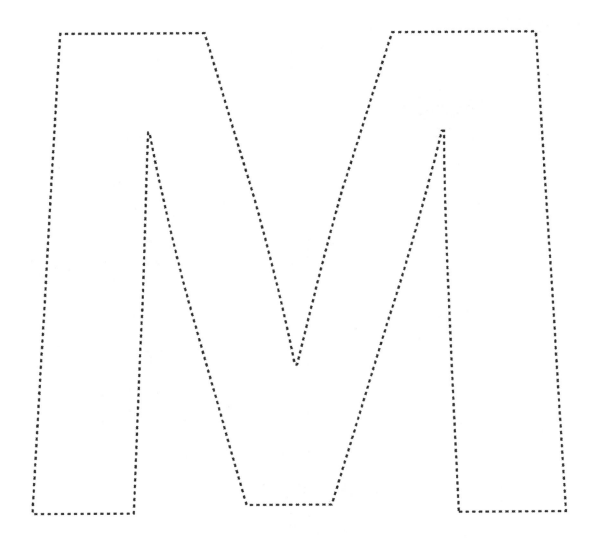

Have the child repeat this twice.

What begins with the Letter M ?

Mailbox

Moon

Maze

Mop

Monkey

Money

Say the name out loud of each picture and listen carefully to the consonant sound of the words that begin with the letter "M." Color it.

Can you tell me what letter this is?

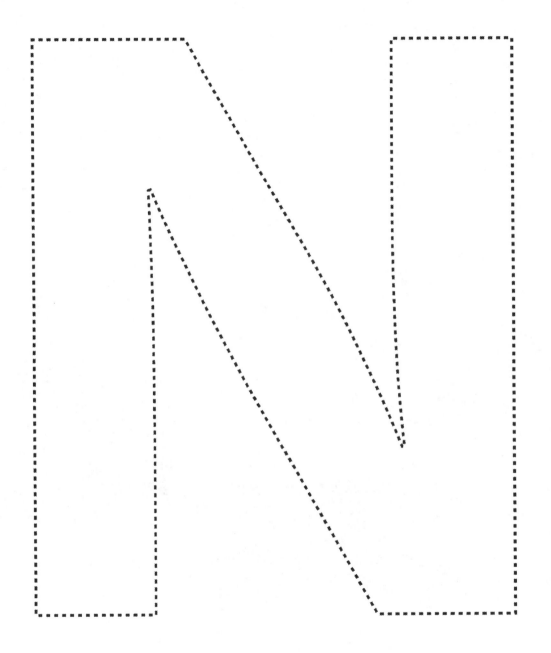

Have the child repeat this twice.

What begins with the Letter N ?

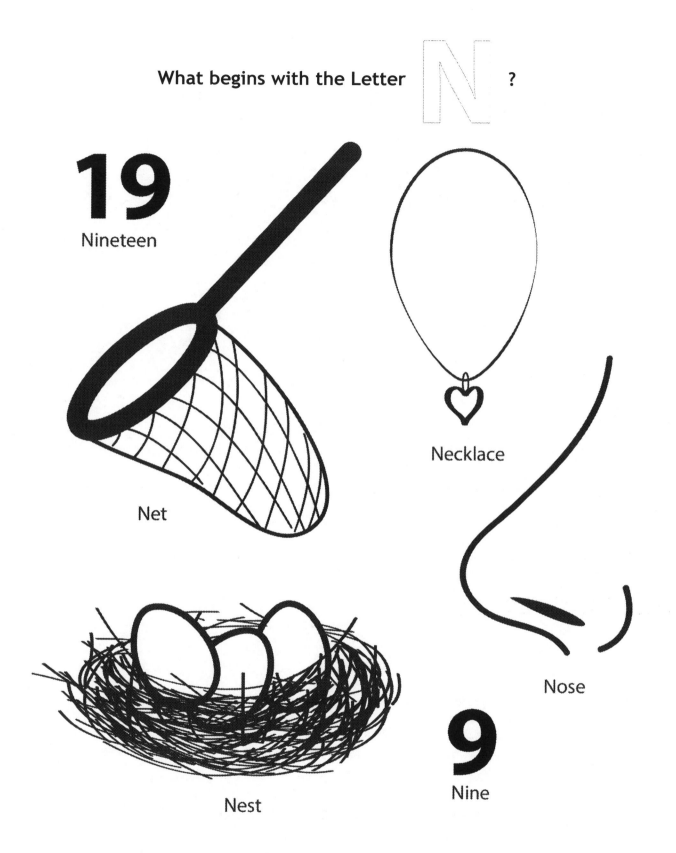

19
Nineteen

Net

Necklace

Nose

Nest

9
Nine

Say the name out loud of each picture and listen carefully to the consonant sound of the words that begin with the letter "N." Color it.

Can you tell me what letter this is?

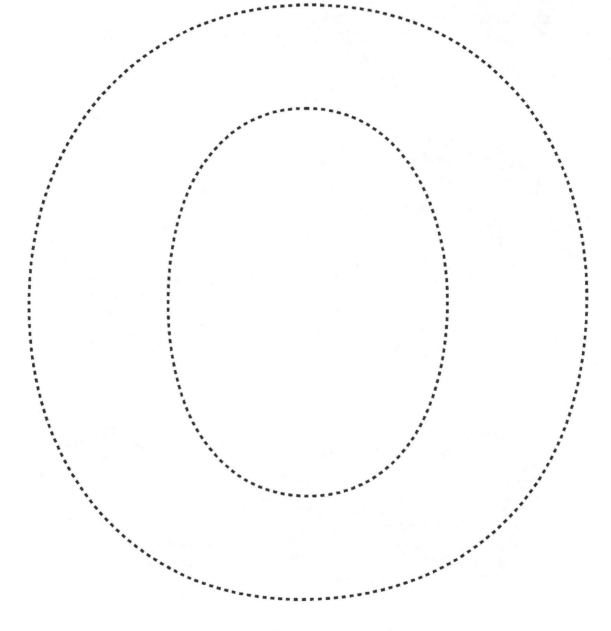

Have the child repeat this twice.

What begins with the Letter O ?

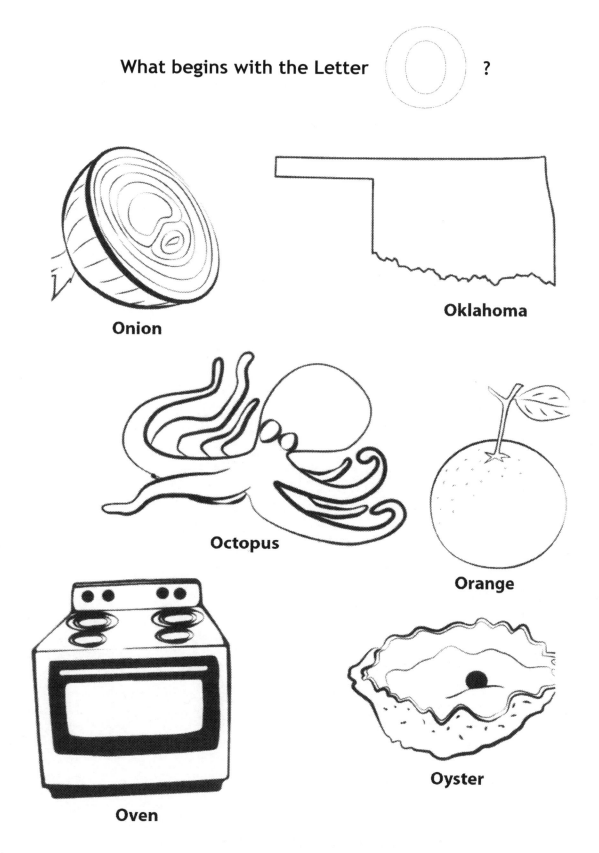

Onion

Oklahoma

Octopus

Orange

Oven

Oyster

Say the name out loud of each picture and listen carefully to the vowel sound of the words that begin with the letter "O." Color it.

Can you tell me what letter this is?

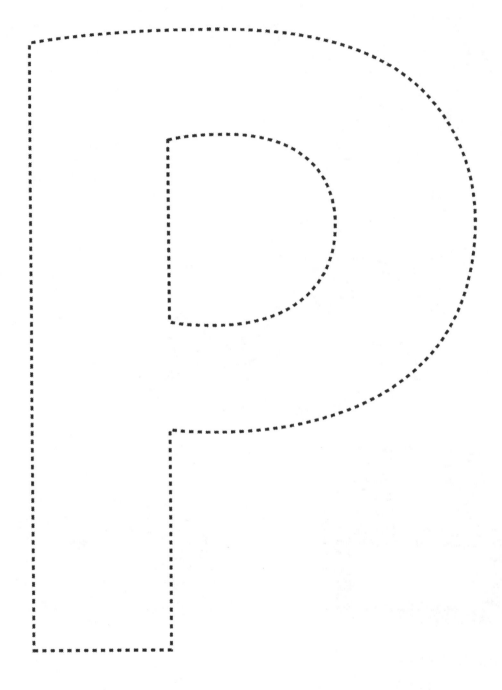

Have the child repeat this twice.

What begins with the Letter P ?

Pie

Pail

Pencil

Pig

Pumpkin

Say the name out loud of each picture and listen carefully to the consonant sound of the words that begin with the letter "P." Color it.

Can you tell me what letter this is?

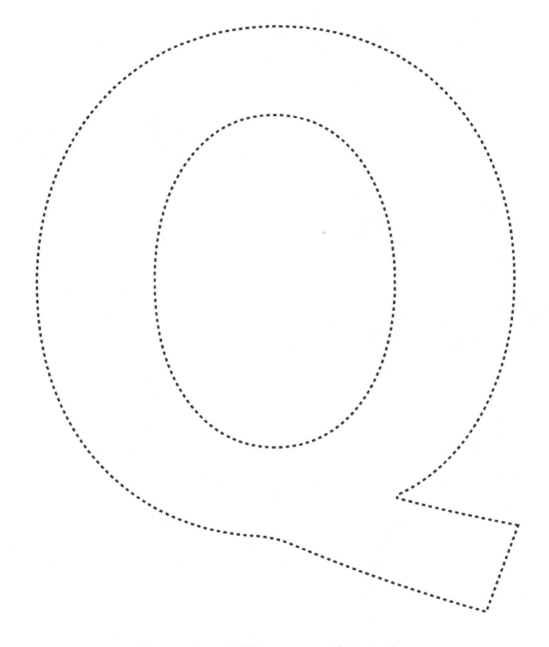

Have the child repeat this twice.

What begins with the Letter Q ?

Question

Quartz

Quarter

Quotes

Quilt

Quail

Say the name out loud of each picture and listen carefully to the consonant sound of the words that begin with the letter "Q." Color it.

Can you tell me what letter this is?

Have the child repeat this twice.

What begins with the Letter R ?

Rose

Ring

Radio

Rabbit

Raspberry

Ruler

Say the name out loud of each picture and listen carefully to the consonant sound of the words that begin with the letter "R." Color it.

Can you tell me what letter this is?

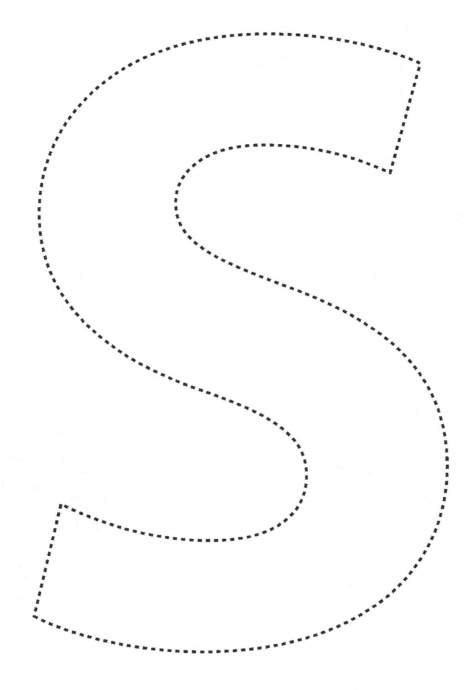

Have the child repeat this twice.

What begins with the Letter S ?

Shark

Snowman

Seven

Sun

Star

Say the name out loud of each picture and listen carefully to the consonant sound of the words that begin with the letter "S." Color it.

Can you tell me what letter this is?

Have the child repeat this twice.

What begins with the Letter T **?**

10
Ten

Top

Telephone

Tree

12
Twelve

Tomato

Tent

2
Two

Say the name out loud of each picture and listen carefully to the consonant sound of the words that begin with the letter "T." Color it.

Can you tell me what letter this is?

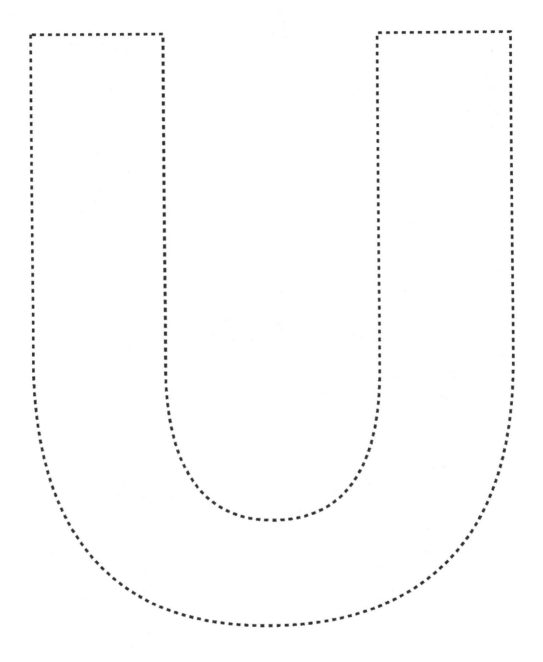

Have the child repeat this twice.

What begins with the Letter U ?

USA

Umbrella

Ukulele

Unicorn

Urn

Say the name out loud of each picture and listen carefully to the vowel sound of the words that begin with the letter "U." Color it.

Can you tell me what letter this is?

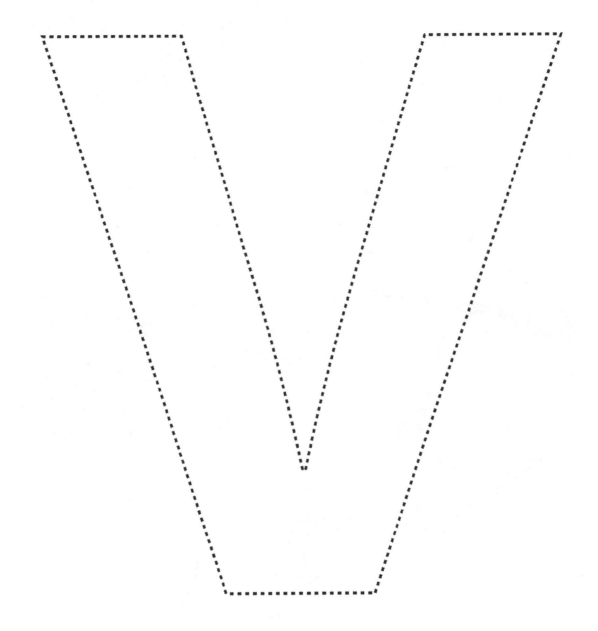

Have the child repeat this twice.

What begins with the Letter V ?

Volley ball

Violin

Vacuum

Volcano

Vase

A E I
U O

Vowels

Say the name out loud of each picture and listen carefully to the consonant sound of the words that begin with the letter "V." Color it.

Can you tell me what letter this is?

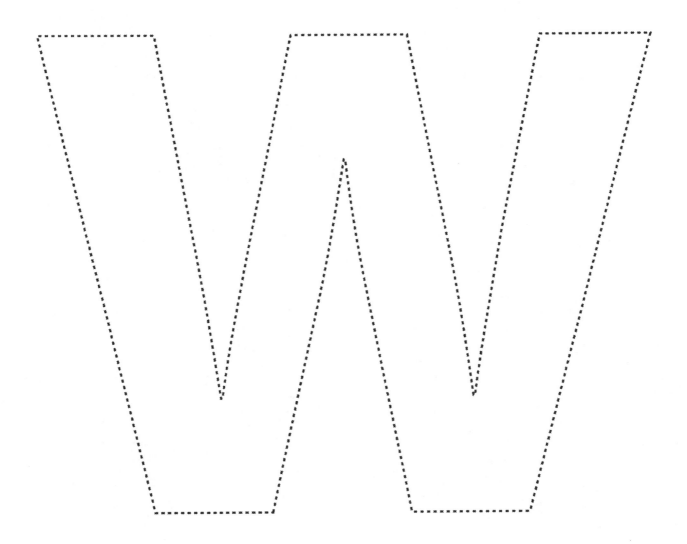

Have the child repeat this twice.

What begins with the Letter W ?

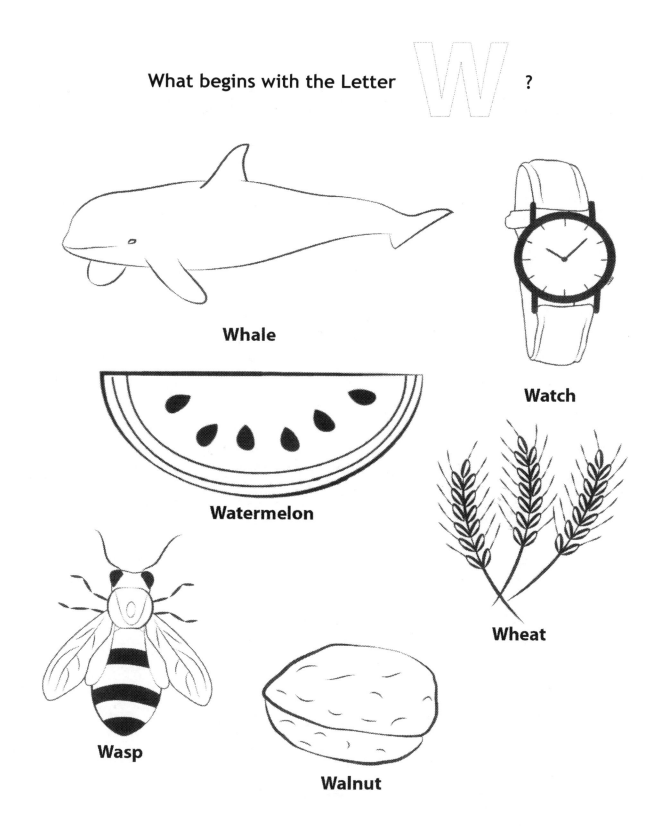

Whale

Watch

Watermelon

Wheat

Wasp

Walnut

Say the name out loud of each picture and listen carefully to the consonant sound of the words that begin with the letter "W." Color it.

Can you tell me what letter this is?

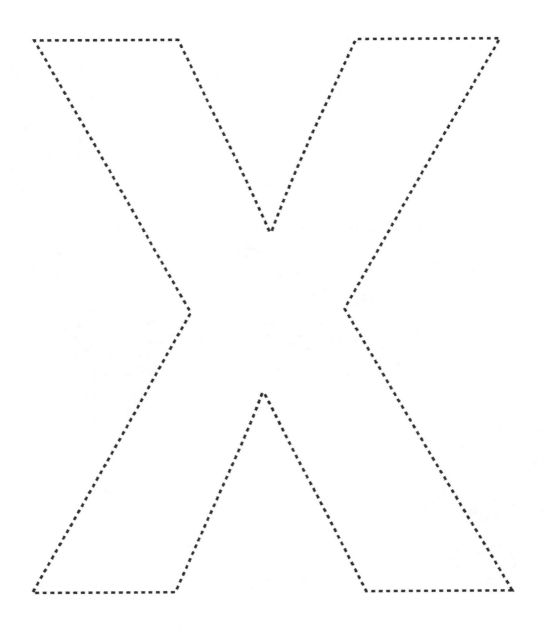

Have the child repeat this twice.

What begins with the Letter X ?

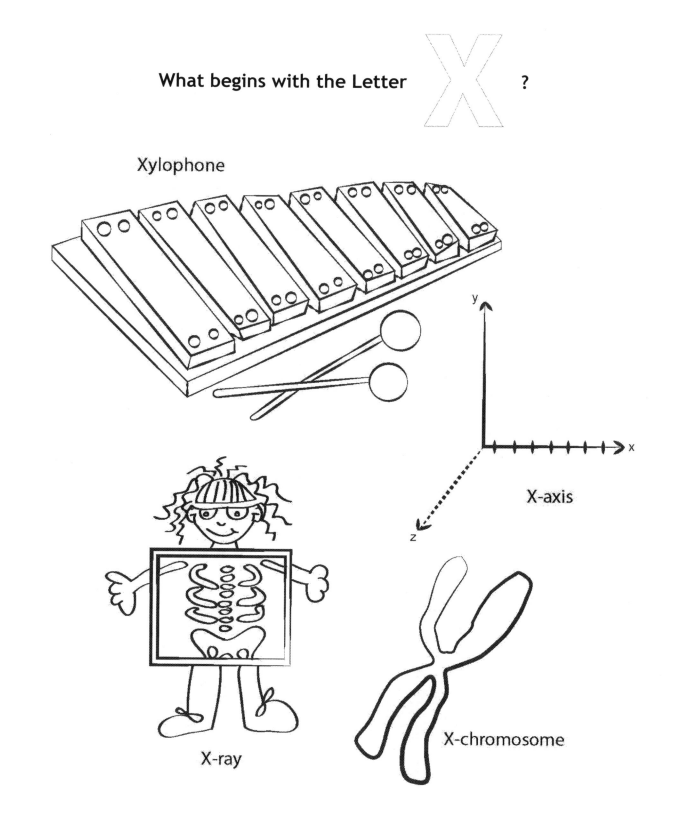

Xylophone

X-axis

X-ray

X-chromosome

Say the name out loud of each picture and listen carefully to the consonant sound of the words that begin with the letter "X." Color it.

Can you tell me what letter this is?

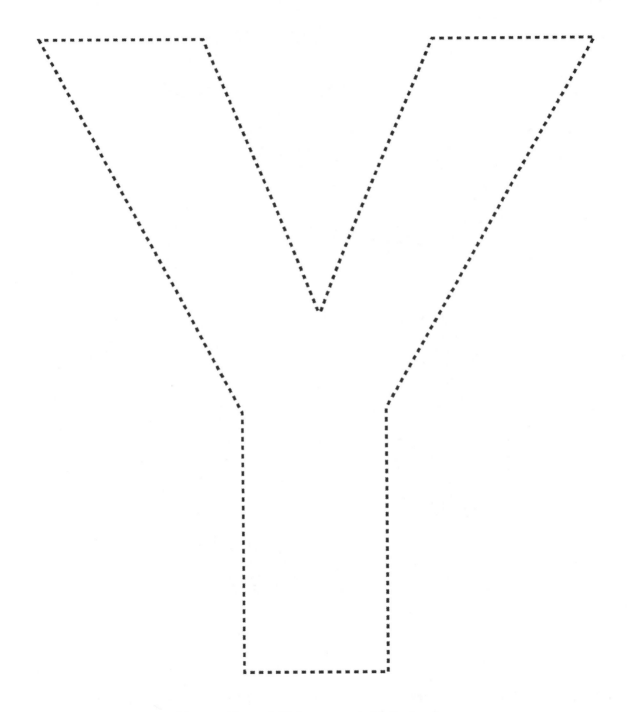

Have the child repeat this twice.

What begins with the Letter Y ?

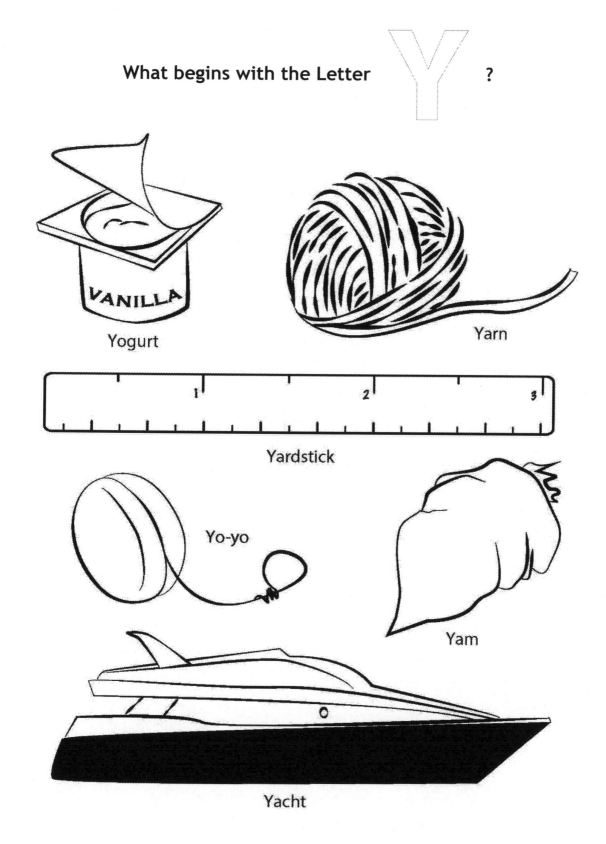

Yogurt

Yarn

Yardstick

Yo-yo

Yam

Yacht

Say the name out loud of each picture and listen carefully to the consonant sound of the words that begin with the letter "Y." Color it.

Can you tell me what letter this is?

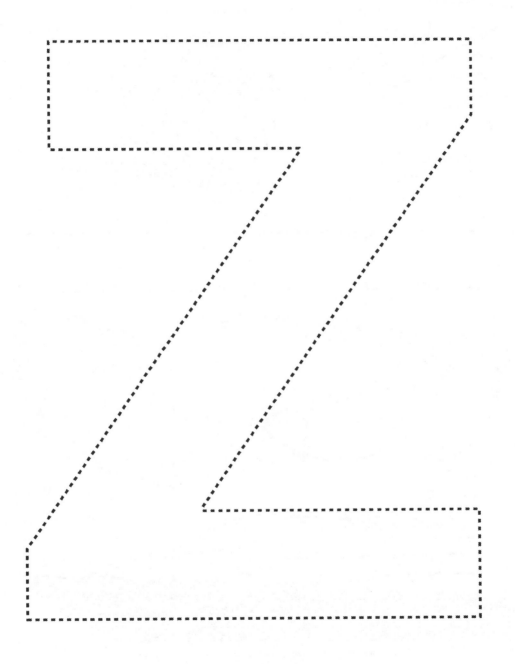

Have the child repeat this twice.

What begins with the Letter Z ?

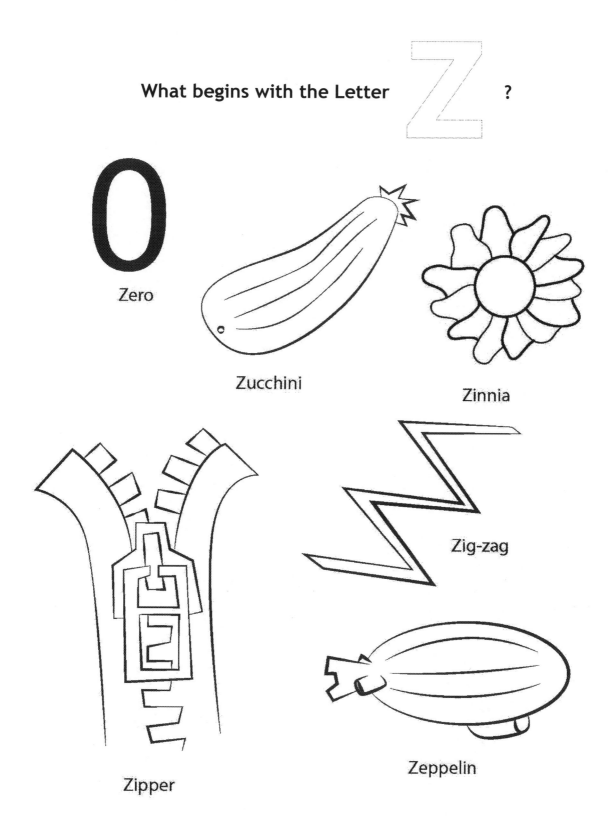

0

Zero

Zucchini

Zinnia

Zig-zag

Zipper

Zeppelin

Say the name out loud of each picture and listen carefully to the consonant sound of the words that begin with the letter "Z." Color it.

SKILLS: TRACE THE LINES
NAME:

SKILLS: TRACE THE LINES
NAME:

SKILLS: ZIGZAG LINES
NAME:

SKILLS: ZIGZAG LINES
NAME:

SKILLS: PARALLEL LINES
NAME:

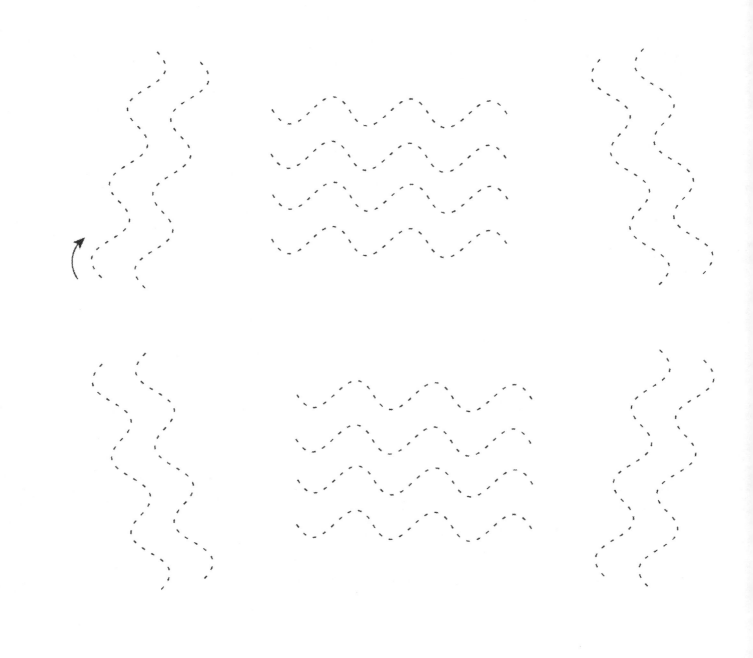

SKILLS: PARALLEL LINES
NAME:

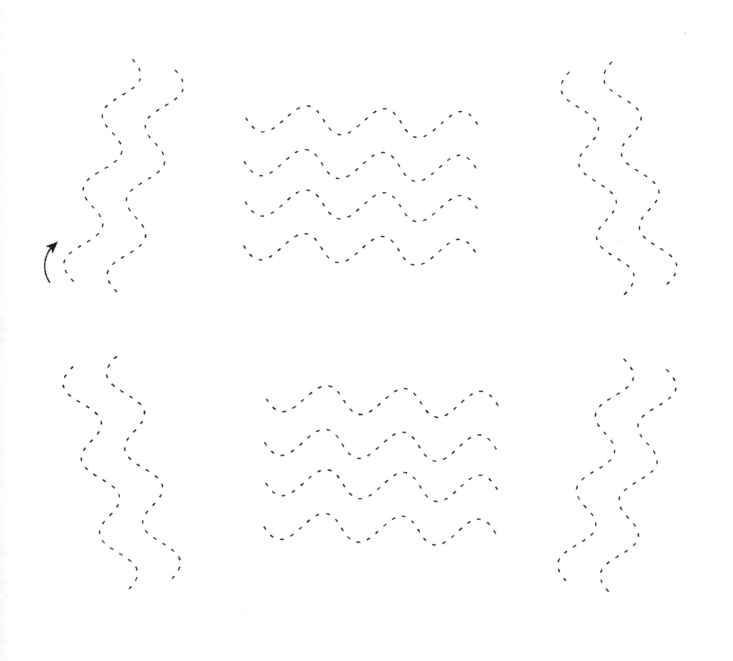

SKILLS: COUNTER-CLOCKWISE MOVEMENT
NAME:

NAME:

SKILLS: CIRCLES
NAME:

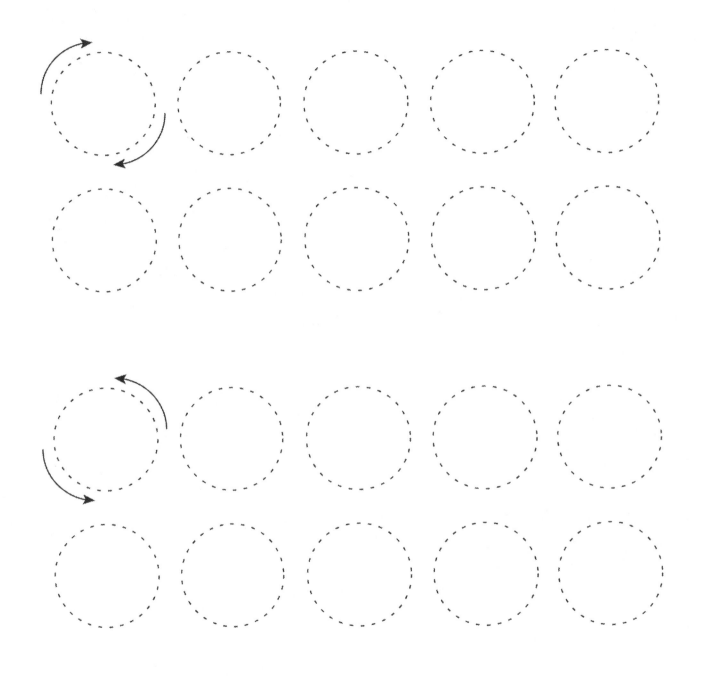

SKILLS: CIRCLES
NAME:

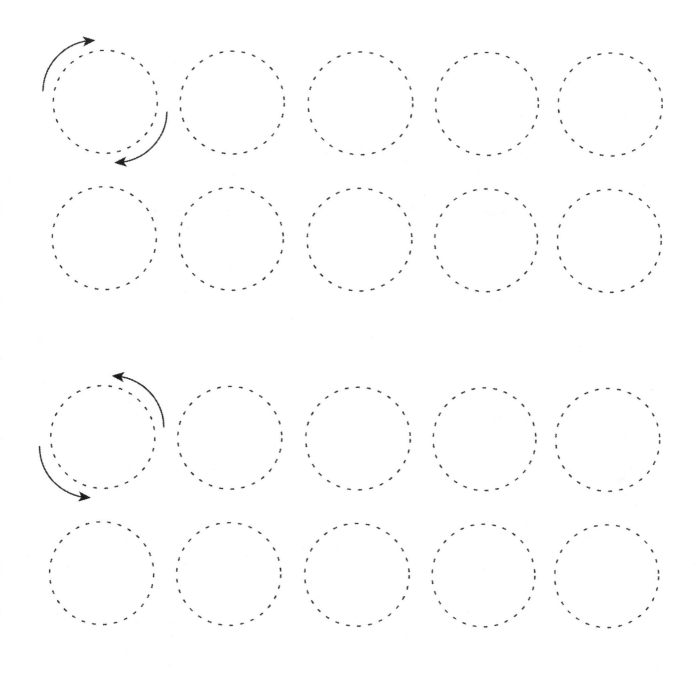

SKILLS: TRACE THE LETTERS
NAME:

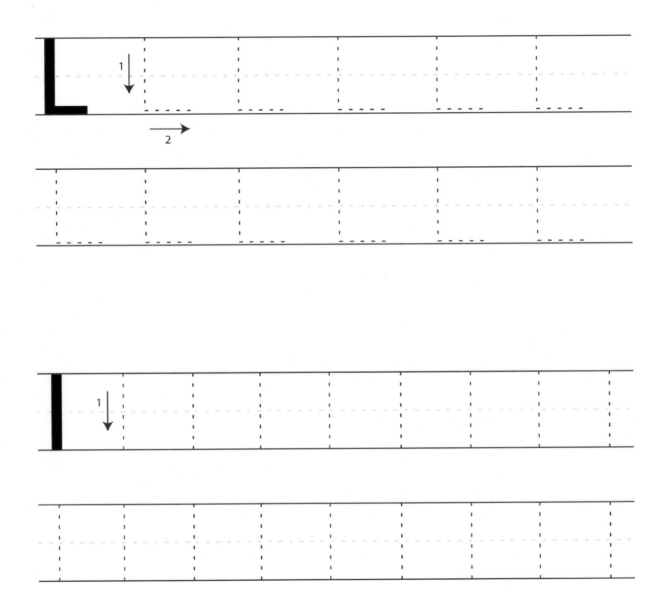

SKILLS: TRACE THE LETTERS
NAME:

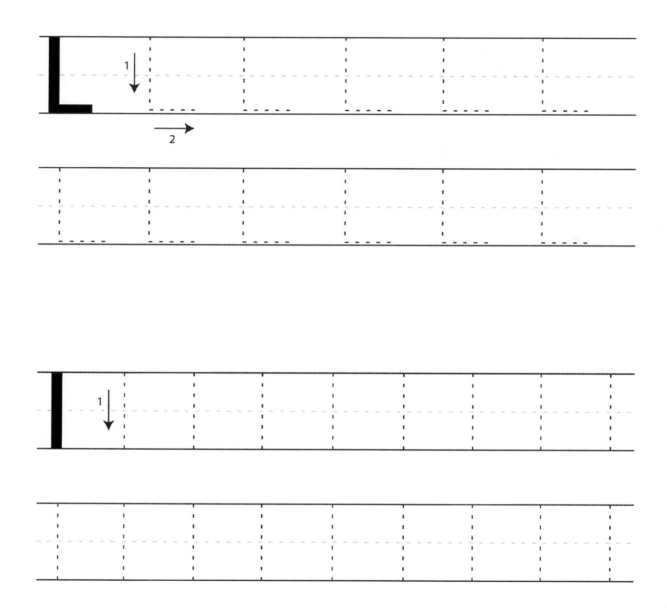

SKILLS: HORIZONTAL AND OPEN CURVES MOVEMENT
NAME:

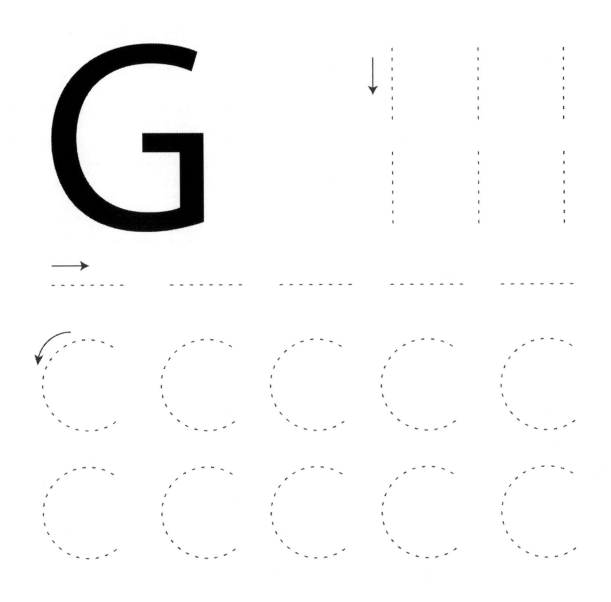

SKILLS: HORIZONTAL AND OPEN CURVES MOVEMENT
NAME:

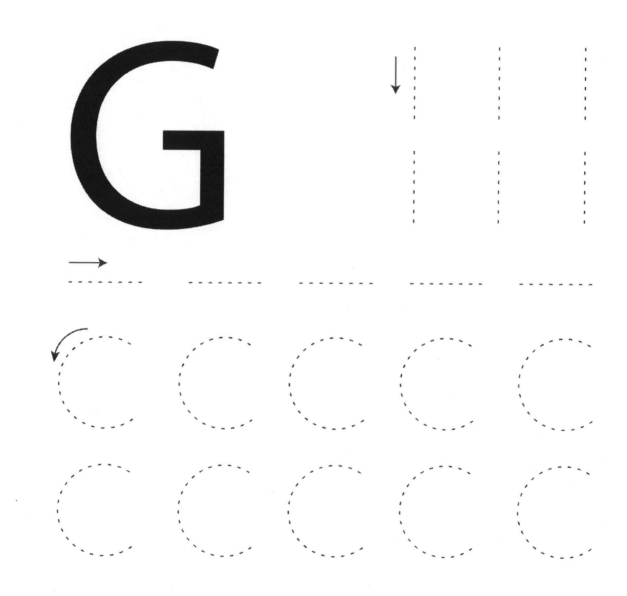